Kathy —
this little book just
validate that you did it
right - - - You are a
good Mom -
            Happy Mother's Day
                    2007
            ♡ Pat

Presented to

_____

From

_____

Date

_____

Love Adds the Chocolate

WRITTEN BY
Linda Andersen

ILLUSTRATED BY
Vicki Wehrman

WATERBROOK
PRESS

LOVE ADDS THE CHOCOLATE
PUBLISHED BY WATERBROOK PRESS
5446 North Academy Boulevard, Suite 200
Colorado Springs, Colorado 80918
A division of Random House, Inc.

ISBN 1-57856-325-9

Library of Congress Cataloging-in-Publication Data
Andersen, Linda, 1940-
   Love adds the chocolate / written by Linda Andersen ; illustrated by Vicki Wehrman.—
   1st ed.
      p. cm.
   ISBN 1-57856-325-9
   1. Christian women—Religious life. I. Wehrman, Vicki, ill. II. Title.
   BV4527 .A49 2000
   242'.643—dc21

                                                                            00-022844

Printed in the United States of America
2000—First Edition

10 9 8 7 6 5 4 3 2 1

Dedicated to Roy,

my husband,

who adds all the chocolate

to my life.

A house

is a house

is a house...

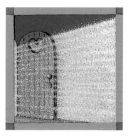

...until love comes through the door, that is.

And love intuitively goes around sprinkling

that special brand of angel dust that transforms

a house into a very special home

for very special people...your family.

Money, of course, can build a charming house,

but only love can furnish it

with a feeling of home.

Money can paint a wall, but only love cares

enough to cover that wall with the handiwork

of children—bouquets, poems, leaves,

and maybe even a crayoned autograph.

Duty can pack an adequate sack lunch,

but love may decide to tuck a little

love note inside.

Money can provide a television set, but love

controls it and cares enough to say no...

and take the guff that comes with it.

Obligation sends children to bed on time,

but love tucks the covers under their chins

and passes out kisses and hugs (even to teenagers!).

Love reminds them of their heavenly Father

and His great love for them.

Duty boils the potatoes, but love adds the parsley...

and the pat of butter...and maybe a scattering

of crushed aromatic herbs.

Obligation can cook a meal, but love embellishes

the table with a potted ivy trailing

around slender candles.

Duty writes many letters, but love tucks a joke

or a picture or a piece of gum inside…

and sends them off with a prayer.

Compulsion keeps a sparkling house,

but love and prayer stand a better chance

of producing a happy family.

Love asks itself, "What else can I do to make

someone else's day easier?" and then does it

with special flair, creativity, joy—

and lots of laughter.

Obligation can pour a glass of milk,

but quite often love will add a little chocolate.

"But the greatest of these is love."

1 Corinthians 13:13